THE MANIFESTATION BLUEPRINT

BY GLENN ROTTMANN, CHT

YOUR VISION IS THE BLUEPRINT FOR WHAT CAN BECOME YOUR REALITY

WATCH A FREE WEBINAR ON HOW TO GET THE MOST OUT OF THE MANIFESTATION BLUEPRINT

FOREWARD

Welcome to **The Manifestation Blueprint**, a transformative guide designed to empower you to manifest the life you've always dreamed of. Through years of personal experience and deep exploration into the power of the subconscious mind, I've discovered that the key to unlocking your greatest potential lies within your own beliefs, actions, and daily intentions. Manifestation is not just a mystical process— it's a blueprint that when followed, can lead to tangible results in all areas of life, from wealth to relationships, health, and personal growth. This book is built on the simple yet profound idea that our subconscious mind is always working— whether we are aware of it or not. By learning how to consciously influence this incredible force through goal setting, affirmations, self-reflection, and mindful awareness, you'll begin to see real change. The Manifestation Blueprint isn't just about wishful thinking. It's about creating a clear pathway for your desires by aligning your **thoughts, beliefs, and actions** with your highest intentions.

Throughout this journey, you'll use these powerful techniques to break free from limiting beliefs, set goals with clarity and purpose, and reinforce them with affirmations that align with your core values. You'll also uncover the magic behind reflection and how small, consistent actions can lead to massive transformation. Manifestation is not just about what you desire; it's about becoming the person who naturally attracts and creates those desires. With faith, expectancy, and desire at the forefront, you'll step into a new reality that reflects your dreams. Whether you're new to the idea of manifestation or looking to refine your practice, "**The Manifestation Blueprint**" offers a practical and spiritual approach that anyone can follow. This is your time to create, to believe, and to become unstoppable.I have one intention in sharing these techniques in the book with you: to create a better life for yourself, filled with your dreams brought to life! -Glenn Rottmann

ABOUT THE AUTHOR

Glenn Rottmann is a dedicated hypnotherapist and personal development coach with a deep passion for helping individuals tap into their subconscious potential to create lasting, positive change. With years of experience working with clients to reprogram limiting beliefs and manifest their desires, Glenn has developed **The Manifestation Blueprint** to share the same tools and insights that have transformed countless lives. His unique blend of spiritual wisdom and practical strategies makes his approach to manifestation accessible to anyone seeking to take control of their life's direction.

In addition to his work as a coach, Glenn is the creator of **The Hypno Vault**, an online platform offering powerful hypnotherapy products designed to help people overcome challenges and reach their goals. His expertise, combined with his dedication to personal growth and transformation, has positioned him as a leading voice in the manifestation and self-help space. His work is now celebrated worldwide, as he is one of the most recognized Hypnotherapists in the world!

HOW "THE MANIFESTATION BLUEPRINT" WORKS

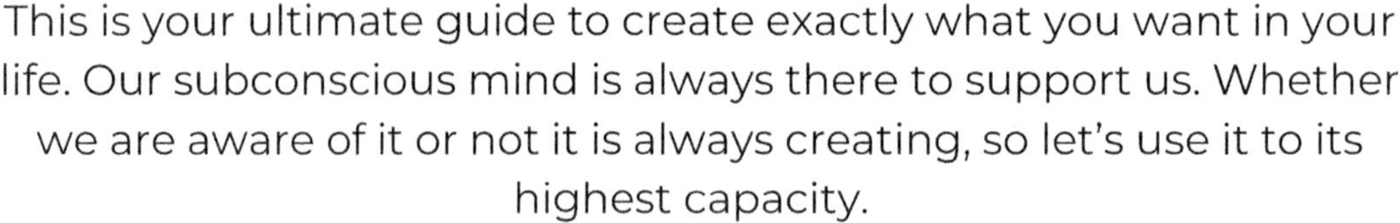

This is your ultimate guide to create exactly what you want in your life. Our subconscious mind is always there to support us. Whether we are aware of it or not it is always creating, so let's use it to its highest capacity.

Some people call it "The Law of Attraction," while others call it "The Law of Creation." In its simplest form, when we define our goals, take consistent action and work with our subconscious minds - we become unstoppable!

We accomplish this by defining our goals, written affirmation, self-reflection, becoming aware of our actions and attaching them to wealth. There is no mistake that thousands of people have achieved their goals and dreams by using
"**The Manifestation Blueprint**."

There is a saying; "Pray as if everything depends upon your Higher Power, work as if everything depends upon you!"

This is where the **magic** of your dreams comes to life!

FAITH IN YOURSELF AND BRINGING YOUR DREAMS TO LIFE IS MADE UP OF DESIRE, BELIEF AND EXPECTANCY.

Desire is the underlying force that starts everything. Underneath every dream and every goal lies that fundamental desire.

Belief is what keeps you going. Belief makes up the gap between desiring something and expecting it to be in your life.

Expectancy this is the end result of the goal that you have put in your sight. Expectancy is simply believing in the fact that you desire this in your life.

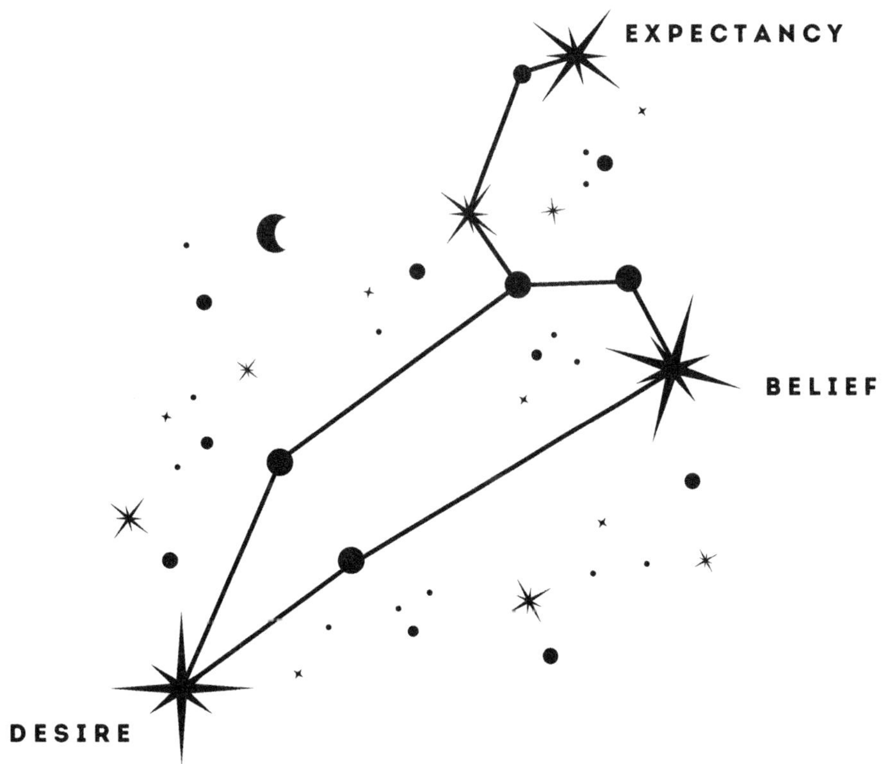

1 - GOALS

The manifestation blueprint is divided into four sections.
It is meant to be done at the **end of the day** before going to bed.

There's a saying:
"Those who don't know where they're going, will probably end up somewhere else."

Let's write down three to five goals that you want to achieve. We will revisit these goals from time to time. Let's give yourself and your subconscious mind a clear vision by writing down your goals. Let's also become clear on "The Why." What are the true reasons you want to achieve these goals in your life?

What purpose will achieving your goals bring you? How will you feel? What will it do for you? How will it change your life and possibly the lives of others?

**WHEN YOU KNOW YOUR WHY...
IT WILL BE YOUR GPS IN TIMES OF DOUBT!**

2 - DIARY OF ACTIONS

How do we spend our time? Success is very easy to find once you measure it. Most people never measure or track how they spend their time, especially when it comes to achieving their goals and dreams.

When it comes to your diary of actions, write down the steps you took that were in alignment with your affirmations, even if they are small steps.

EVERY SUCCESSFUL JOURNEY STARTS WITH SMALL CONSISTENT STEPS!

3 - AFFIRMATIONS

"DO THEY REALLY WORK OR IS IT JUST WISHFUL THINKING?"

"WHAT IF I DON'T BELIEVE WHAT I AM WRITING?"

"I HAVE TRIED THEM BEFORE AND THEY DIDN'T WORK."

Yes, they work when done in a way that aligns with our belief system. To affirm means to confirm that something is true. The purpose of an affirmation is to make something familiar that is not in your life yet; so when you attract and create it, it feels natural. This way, you accept it instead of sabotaging it. Through written affirmation, we are going to affirm exactly what it is you want to attract into your life.

Writing it in the **present tense** gives your subconscious mind a feeling of familiarity. This will influence your actions, intentions and beliefs in a way to create exactly what you want. Perhaps something even better!

If you don't believe the affirmation you are writing, let's **shift** the language.

"I CHOOSE TO BELIEVE...

AFFIRMATION EXAMPLES

Instead of: I am a multi-millionaire
(do you genuinely believe that?)

Write: I choose to believe that I am taking the right actions each day that lead to my financial freedom!
(resistance fades, and the mind can accept it)

Instead of: I have the perfect healthy body at the ideal weight. (do you?)

Write: I am increasingly committed every day to nurturing my health and creating a fit, healthy body and lifestyle! (resistance fades, allowing acceptance)

Instead of: I want to be in a happy relationship.

Write: Happy and loving relationships are a natural part of my life; they effortlessly find me.

Instead of: I don't let fear control me anymore.

Write: I possess the courage and trust to tackle and succeed in any challenge I encounter. Or: I choose to believe that I can face any challenge that arises.

Instead of: I'm not sick with (insert the medical issue) anymore.

Write: My body is healing and knows exactly how to overcome this (insert the medical issue). Or: I am in the process of healing my body and attracting the right support for my recovery.

We specifically use the word "this" instead of "my" for negative issues. For example, say "this anxiety" instead of "my anxiety," or "this heartache" instead of "my heartache."

WE MUST NOT CLAIM OUR LIMITATIONS BY USING "MY."

MY FAVORITE AFFIRMATIONS

USE THESE EXAMPLES TO SPARK YOUR CREATIVE ENERGY:

I CHOOSE TO BELIEVE THAT THIS WORLD IS A BEAUTIFUL PLACE AND I FIND JOY EVERYWHERE I LOOK.

EACH AND EVERY DAY AND EACH AND EVERY WAY, MY LIFE IS BETTER AND BETTER.

I TRUST MY ABILITIES AND I CHOOSE TO BELIEVE THAT I CAN TRUST THE CHOICES THAT I MAKE, RELEASING THE NEED TO EVER SECOND-GUESS MYSELF.

THE MORE MONEY I MAKE THE MORE COMFORTABLE
I AM MAKING MONEY. MILLION DOLLAR IDEAS, OPPORTUNITIES AND ACTIONS FLOW INTO MY LIFE.

I'M IN THE PROCESS OF BUILDING A BEAUTIFUL LIFE FULL OF HEALTHY FRIENDS,RELATIONSHIPS AND BEAUTIFUL EXPERIENCES.

SOMETHING WONDERFUL IS GOING TO HAPPEN TO ME TOMORROW!

WHEN IT COMES TO AFFIRMATIONS,
NOT EVEN THE SKY IS THE LIMIT!

4 - REFLECTION

There are only three choices with every new day. We can either **get better, get worse or stay the same**. Taking personal reflection at the end of each day, by recognizing one thing you could improve upon is the key to growth.

This is not about self-judgment; this is about having a growth mindset. It could be something small about how you react or act in general, or even a bigger personality trait you would like to shift.

"I'M IN THE PROCESS OF BUILDING A BEAUTIFUL LIFE FULL OF HEALTHY FRIENDS, RELATIONSHIPS AND BEAUTIFUL EXPERIENCES."

5 - PAYING YOURSELF

We all know that **money** is a motivating factor. The $ymbol of money and the meaning of money speak directly to our subconscious mind. By creating a mental reward system based around the symbols of money, we achieve extraordinary results.

Because money is such an important factor in our lives, **our relationship to money either motivates us or keeps us feeling stuck.** Using money as a way to affirm and create our dreams is one of the biggest keys in manifesting.

Every time you see the blank check in your journal, write yourself a check! For your first check **double the amount** that you have in your bank account right now. Then **add 50%** for each check that you will write to yourself after that.

THIS WORKS ON SO MANY LEVELS

5 - PAYING YOURSELF (CONTINUED)

Example:

If you have $10,000 in your bank account right now. Write your first check for: $20,000

$10,000 + $10,000 = $20,000

For your next check take the $20,000 amount and add 50%. Making this check out for $30,000

$20,000 + $10,000 = $30,000

For your next check take the $30,000 amount and add 50%. Making this check out for $45,000

$30,000 + $15,000 = $45,000

Then just keep adding 50% to each check as you move from journal to journal. You will be amazed at how writing these checks will start to affect the way you think about money.

SIGN YOUR CHECK TO SEAL YOUR INTENTIONS

6 - MIRROR NUMBERS

The world is made up of energy, and there is a frequency for everything. When you zoom in on a microscope, even solid objects have atoms that vibrate. Let's use this to our favor by checking in on our own emotional energy, by utilizing the power of mirror numbers.

Mirror Numbers (some call them Angel Numbers) are when the times on a clock mirror each other.

FILL IN YOUR MIRROR NUMBERS

HERE ARE SOME EXAMPLES USING A 24-HOUR CLOCK:

00:00, 01:10, 02:20, 03:30, 04:40, 05:50, 10:01, 11:11, 12:21, 13:31, 14:41, 15:51, 20:02, 21:12, 22:22, 23:32

In many cultures and spiritual practices, specific numbers are believed to hold unique vibrations or energies. This can influence your life in many positive ways. Understandably, the significance of these numbers may be subjective from person to person. But why not use this to our favor?

6 - MIRROR NUMBERS

I want you to **choose two times every day, one in the morning and one in the afternoon/evening**. You can use the same number for both am and pm if you're using a 12 hour clock. During these times, **self-reflect, think about your intentions, review your mindset, check your energy** and say a couple of your affirmations to yourself.

This entire process should only take 2 to 3 minutes at most, but it is such an important thing to do. Keep yourself in alignment with achieving your goals and using this gift we call the universe to work in your favor.

I find it best to set a reminder on your cell phone about a minute or two before your mirror numbers come up; that way you can prepare yourself to start right on time.

FOR EXAMPLE: IF YOU CHOOSE 10:01 AS YOUR MIRROR NUMBER, SET YOUR ALARM FOR A FEW MINUTES BEFORE.

7 - CONSISTENCY

I want you to remember life is about progress and not perfection. The more consistent you are, the quicker you will truly achieve your goals and dreams. If you miss a day, just pick it up the next day. If you miss a mirror number reflection time, catch it on the next mirror number.

You don't have to do it perfectly...

JUST DO IT!

JOURNALING

DATE: ___/___/___

LET'S MAKE A BLUEPRINT OF YOU WHAT YOU WANT IN YOUR LIFE

WRITE DOWN THREE TO FIVE GOALS THAT YOU WANT TO ACHIEVE:

DEFINE YOUR "WHY" FOR THESE GOALS: (BE SPECIFIC)

EVENING JOURNALING

DATE: __/__/__

WRITE DOWN ANY STEPS YOU TOOK TOWARDS YOUR GOALS TODAY

REFLECTION:

ONE THING YOU COULD IMPROVE UPON FROM TODAY:

AFFIRMATIONS:

DATE: __/__/__

EACH AND EVERY DAY IN EACH AND EVERY WAY
MY LIFE IS BETTER AND BETTER

EVENING JOURNALING

DATE: ___/___/___

WRITE DOWN ANY STEPS YOU TOOK TOWARDS YOUR GOALS TODAY

REFLECTION:

ONE THING YOU COULD IMPROVE UPON FROM TODAY:

AFFIRMATIONS: DATE: ___/___/___

EACH AND EVERY DAY IN EACH AND EVERY WAY
MY LIFE IS BETTER AND BETTER

EVENING JOURNALING

DATE: __/__/__

WRITE DOWN ANY STEPS YOU TOOK TOWARDS YOUR GOALS TODAY

REFLECTION:

ONE THING YOU COULD IMPROVE UPON FROM TODAY:

AFFIRMATIONS:

DATE: ___/___/___

EACH AND EVERY DAY IN EACH AND EVERY WAY
MY LIFE IS BETTER AND BETTER

EVENING JOURNALING

DATE: __/__/__

WRITE DOWN ANY STEPS YOU TOOK TOWARDS YOUR GOALS TODAY

REFLECTION:

ONE THING YOU COULD IMPROVE UPON FROM TODAY:

AFFIRMATIONS: DATE: __/__/__

EACH AND EVERY DAY IN EACH AND EVERY WAY
MY LIFE IS BETTER AND BETTER

EVENING JOURNALING

DATE: ___/___/___

WRITE DOWN ANY STEPS YOU TOOK TOWARDS YOUR GOALS TODAY

REFLECTION:

ONE THING YOU COULD IMPROVE UPON FROM TODAY:

AFFIRMATIONS:

DATE: ___/___/___

EACH AND EVERY DAY IN EACH AND EVERY WAY
MY LIFE IS BETTER AND BETTER

EVENING JOURNALING

DATE: ___/___/___

WRITE DOWN ANY STEPS YOU TOOK TOWARDS YOUR GOALS TODAY

REFLECTION:

ONE THING YOU COULD IMPROVE UPON FROM TODAY:

AFFIRMATIONS: DATE: __/__/__

EACH AND EVERY DAY IN EACH AND EVERY WAY
MY LIFE IS BETTER AND BETTER

EVENING JOURNALING

DATE: ___/___/___

WRITE DOWN ANY STEPS YOU TOOK TOWARDS YOUR GOALS TODAY

REFLECTION:

ONE THING YOU COULD IMPROVE UPON FROM TODAY:

AFFIRMATIONS: DATE: ___/___/___

EACH AND EVERY DAY IN EACH AND EVERY WAY
MY LIFE IS BETTER AND BETTER

IT'S TIME TO PAY YOURSELF

DATE

PAY TO THE ORDER OF $

DOLLARS

MEMO *I attract abundance*

0 1 1 0 1 0 0 1 0 2 2 0 1 1 1 1 1 2 2 1 1 4 4 1

WRITE A CHECK TO YOURSELF FOR DOUBLE THE AMOUNT OF WHAT YOU HAVE IN YOUR CHECKING ACCOUNT.

Each time you write a new check with an increased amount, you are actively signaling to your subconscious that you are ready to welcome more abundance into your life. As the numbers grow larger, so does your capacity to attract wealth, success, and fulfillment.

This practice isn't just about money—it's about shifting your mindset to embrace the limitless possibilities available to you. With every check, you're reinforcing the belief that your life can expand in ways that bring you greater abundance and deeper satisfaction. Watch how your reality begins to reflect the prosperity your creating.

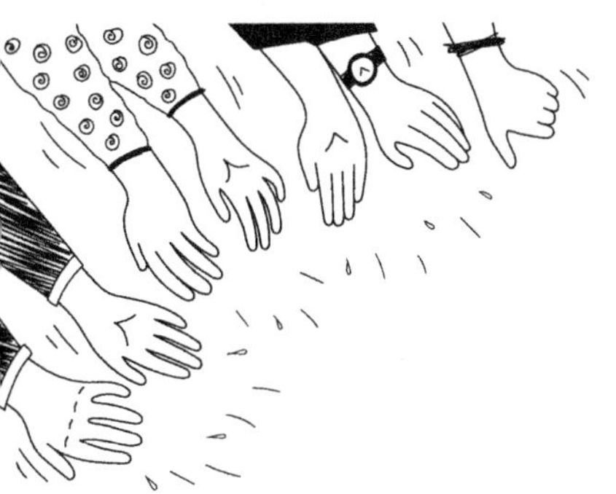

I AM THE CREATOR OF MY LIFE SHAPING MY REALITY EVERY DAY.

TO **LIVE** A LIFE THAT MOST PEOPLE NEVER GET TO **EXPERIENCE**, YOU MUST **DO THINGS** THAT MOST PEOPLE ARE NOT WILLING TO DO

EVENING JOURNALING

DATE: ___/___/___

WRITE DOWN ANY STEPS YOU TOOK TOWARDS YOUR GOALS TODAY

REFLECTION:

ONE THING YOU COULD IMPROVE UPON FROM TODAY:

AFFIRMATIONS:

DATE: ___/___/___

EACH AND EVERY DAY IN EACH AND EVERY WAY
MY LIFE IS BETTER AND BETTER

EVENING JOURNALING

DATE: ___/___/___

WRITE DOWN ANY STEPS YOU TOOK TOWARDS YOUR GOALS TODAY

REFLECTION:

ONE THING YOU COULD IMPROVE UPON FROM TODAY:

AFFIRMATIONS:

DATE: __/__/__

EACH AND EVERY DAY IN EACH AND EVERY WAY
MY LIFE IS BETTER AND BETTER

EVENING JOURNALING

DATE: ___/___/___

WRITE DOWN ANY STEPS YOU TOOK TOWARDS YOUR GOALS TODAY

REFLECTION:

ONE THING YOU COULD IMPROVE UPON FROM TODAY:

AFFIRMATIONS:

DATE: ___/___/___

EACH AND EVERY DAY IN EACH AND EVERY WAY
MY LIFE IS BETTER AND BETTER

EVENING JOURNALING

DATE: __/__/__

WRITE DOWN ANY STEPS YOU TOOK TOWARDS YOUR GOALS TODAY

REFLECTION:

ONE THING YOU COULD IMPROVE UPON FROM TODAY:

AFFIRMATIONS:

DATE: ___/___/___

EACH AND EVERY DAY IN EACH AND EVERY WAY
MY LIFE IS BETTER AND BETTER

EVENING JOURNALING

DATE: ___/___/___

WRITE DOWN ANY STEPS YOU TOOK TOWARDS YOUR GOALS TODAY

REFLECTION:

ONE THING YOU COULD IMPROVE UPON FROM TODAY:

AFFIRMATIONS:

DATE: ___/___/___

EACH AND EVERY DAY IN EACH AND EVERY WAY
MY LIFE IS BETTER AND BETTER

EVENING JOURNALING

DATE: ___/___/___

WRITE DOWN ANY STEPS YOU TOOK TOWARDS YOUR GOALS TODAY

REFLECTION:

ONE THING YOU COULD IMPROVE UPON FROM TODAY:

AFFIRMATIONS: DATE: ___/___/___

EACH AND EVERY DAY IN EACH AND EVERY WAY
MY LIFE IS BETTER AND BETTER

EVENING JOURNALING

DATE: ___/___/___

WRITE DOWN ANY STEPS YOU TOOK TOWARDS YOUR GOALS TODAY

REFLECTION:

ONE THING YOU COULD IMPROVE UPON FROM TODAY:

AFFIRMATIONS:

DATE: ___/___/___

EACH AND EVERY DAY IN EACH AND EVERY WAY
MY LIFE IS BETTER AND BETTER

IT'S TIME TO PAY YOURSELF BY FILLING OUT THIS CHECK!

DATE

PAY TO THE ORDER OF $

DOLLARS

MEMO *I attract abundance*

0 1 1 0 1 0 0 1 0 2 2 0 1 1 1 1 1 2 2 1 1 4 4 1

Time to celebrate! Write another check to yourself, this time **increasing the amount by 50%** from the balance of your **previous** check.

YOUR SUBCONSCIOUS MIND LOVES WHEN YOU USE MONEY AS A SYMBOL OF YOUR SUCCESS!

IT'S THE LITTLE THINGS YOU DO CONSISTENTLY
THAT SHAPE THE LIFE OF YOUR DREAMS

DESIRE - BELIEF - EXPECTANCY

EVENING JOURNALING

DATE: ___/___/___

WRITE DOWN ANY STEPS YOU TOOK TOWARDS YOUR GOALS TODAY

REFLECTION:

ONE THING YOU COULD IMPROVE UPON FROM TODAY:

AFFIRMATIONS: DATE: ___/___/___

EACH AND EVERY DAY IN EACH AND EVERY WAY
MY LIFE IS BETTER AND BETTER

EVENING JOURNALING

DATE: ___/___/___

WRITE DOWN ANY STEPS YOU TOOK TOWARDS YOUR GOALS TODAY

REFLECTION:

ONE THING YOU COULD IMPROVE UPON FROM TODAY:

AFFIRMATIONS:

DATE: ___/___/___

EACH AND EVERY DAY IN EACH AND EVERY WAY
MY LIFE IS BETTER AND BETTER

EVENING JOURNALING

DATE: ___/___/___

WRITE DOWN ANY STEPS YOU TOOK TOWARDS YOUR GOALS TODAY

REFLECTION:

ONE THING YOU COULD IMPROVE UPON FROM TODAY:

AFFIRMATIONS:

DATE: ___/___/___

EACH AND EVERY DAY IN EACH AND EVERY WAY
MY LIFE IS BETTER AND BETTER

EVENING JOURNALING

DATE: ___/___/___

WRITE DOWN ANY STEPS YOU TOOK TOWARDS YOUR GOALS TODAY

REFLECTION:

ONE THING YOU COULD IMPROVE UPON FROM TODAY:

AFFIRMATIONS: DATE: ___/___/___

EACH AND EVERY DAY IN EACH AND EVERY WAY
MY LIFE IS BETTER AND BETTER

EVENING JOURNALING

DATE: ___/___/___

WRITE DOWN ANY STEPS YOU TOOK TOWARDS YOUR GOALS TODAY

REFLECTION:

ONE THING YOU COULD IMPROVE UPON FROM TODAY:

AFFIRMATIONS: DATE: ___/___/___

EACH AND EVERY DAY IN EACH AND EVERY WAY
MY LIFE IS BETTER AND BETTER

EVENING JOURNALING

DATE: ___/___/___

WRITE DOWN ANY STEPS YOU TOOK TOWARDS YOUR GOALS TODAY

REFLECTION:

ONE THING YOU COULD IMPROVE UPON FROM TODAY:

AFFIRMATIONS:

DATE: __/__/__

EACH AND EVERY DAY IN EACH AND EVERY WAY
MY LIFE IS BETTER AND BETTER

EVENING JOURNALING

DATE: ___/___/___

WRITE DOWN ANY STEPS YOU TOOK TOWARDS YOUR GOALS TODAY

REFLECTION:

ONE THING YOU COULD IMPROVE UPON FROM TODAY:

AFFIRMATIONS:

DATE: ___/___/___

EACH AND EVERY DAY IN EACH AND EVERY WAY
MY LIFE IS BETTER AND BETTER

IT'S TIME TO PAY YOURSELF BY FILLING OUT THIS CHECK!

DATE

PAY TO THE ORDER OF $

DOLLARS

MEMO *I attract abundance*

0 1 1 0 1 0 0 1 0 2 2 0 1 1 1 1 1 2 2 1 1 4 4 1

Time to celebrate! Write another check to yourself, this time **increasing the amount by 50%** from the balance of your **previous** check.

YOUR SUBCONSCIOUS MIND LOVES WHEN YOU USE MONEY AS A SYMBOL OF YOUR SUCCESS!

THE THE ONLY LIMITS ARE THE
ONES THAT YOU SET IN YOUR MIND

EMBRACE THE JOUREY

EVENING JOURNALING

DATE: ___/___/___

WRITE DOWN ANY STEPS YOU TOOK TOWARDS YOUR GOALS TODAY

REFLECTION:

ONE THING YOU COULD IMPROVE UPON FROM TODAY:

AFFIRMATIONS:

DATE: ___/___/___

EACH AND EVERY DAY IN EACH AND EVERY WAY
MY LIFE IS BETTER AND BETTER

EVENING JOURNALING

DATE: ___/___/___

WRITE DOWN ANY STEPS YOU TOOK TOWARDS YOUR GOALS TODAY

REFLECTION:

ONE THING YOU COULD IMPROVE UPON FROM TODAY:

AFFIRMATIONS:

DATE: ___/___/___

EACH AND EVERY DAY IN EACH AND EVERY WAY
MY LIFE IS BETTER AND BETTER

EVENING JOURNALING

DATE: ___/___/___

WRITE DOWN ANY STEPS YOU TOOK TOWARDS YOUR GOALS TODAY

REFLECTION:

ONE THING YOU COULD IMPROVE UPON FROM TODAY:

AFFIRMATIONS:

DATE: ___/___/___

EACH AND EVERY DAY IN EACH AND EVERY WAY
MY LIFE IS BETTER AND BETTER

EVENING JOURNALING

DATE: ___/___/___

WRITE DOWN ANY STEPS YOU TOOK TOWARDS YOUR GOALS TODAY

REFLECTION:

ONE THING YOU COULD IMPROVE UPON FROM TODAY:

AFFIRMATIONS: DATE: ___/___/___

EACH AND EVERY DAY IN EACH AND EVERY WAY
MY LIFE IS BETTER AND BETTER

EVENING JOURNALING

DATE: ___/___/___

WRITE DOWN ANY STEPS YOU TOOK TOWARDS YOUR GOALS TODAY

REFLECTION:

ONE THING YOU COULD IMPROVE UPON FROM TODAY:

AFFIRMATIONS:

DATE: ___/___/___

EACH AND EVERY DAY IN EACH AND EVERY WAY
MY LIFE IS BETTER AND BETTER

EVENING JOURNALING

DATE: __/__/__

WRITE DOWN ANY STEPS YOU TOOK TOWARDS YOUR GOALS TODAY

REFLECTION:

ONE THING YOU COULD IMPROVE UPON FROM TODAY:

AFFIRMATIONS: DATE: ___/___/___

EACH AND EVERY DAY IN EACH AND EVERY WAY
MY LIFE IS BETTER AND BETTER

EVENING JOURNALING

DATE: ___/___/___

WRITE DOWN ANY STEPS YOU TOOK TOWARDS YOUR GOALS TODAY

REFLECTION:

ONE THING YOU COULD IMPROVE UPON FROM TODAY:

AFFIRMATIONS:

DATE: ___/___/___

EACH AND EVERY DAY IN EACH AND EVERY WAY
MY LIFE IS BETTER AND BETTER

IT'S TIME TO PAY YOURSELF BY FILLING OUT THIS CHECK!

DATE

PAY TO THE ORDER OF $

DOLLARS

MEMO *I attract abundance*

0 1 1 0 1 0 0 1 0 2 2 0 1 1 1 1 1 2 2 1 1 4 4 1

Time to celebrate! Write another check to yourself, this time **increasing the amount by 50%** from the balance of your **previous** check.

YOUR SUBCONSCIOUS MIND LOVES WHEN YOU USE MONEY AS A SYMBOL OF YOUR SUCCESS!

HAVE THERE BEEN ANY CHANGES?

LET'S CHECK IN!

Now that you've been journaling, visualizing, and taking action, have you noticed any changes? Take a moment to reflect—do your goals need to be redefined, adjusted, or shifted? Or perhaps you're happy with them as they are. It's natural for priorities to evolve during this journey, and maybe you've even achieved some goals and are ready to set new ones.

YOUR GOALS

YOUR REASONS

EVENING JOURNALING

DATE: ___/___/___

WRITE DOWN ANY STEPS YOU TOOK TOWARDS YOUR GOALS TODAY

REFLECTION:

ONE THING YOU COULD IMPROVE UPON FROM TODAY:

AFFIRMATIONS:

DATE: ___/___/___

EACH AND EVERY DAY IN EACH AND EVERY WAY
MY LIFE IS BETTER AND BETTER

EVENING JOURNALING

DATE: ___/___/___

WRITE DOWN ANY STEPS YOU TOOK TOWARDS YOUR GOALS TODAY

REFLECTION:

ONE THING YOU COULD IMPROVE UPON FROM TODAY:

AFFIRMATIONS: DATE: ___/___/___

EACH AND EVERY DAY IN EACH AND EVERY WAY
MY LIFE IS BETTER AND BETTER

EVENING JOURNALING

DATE: ___/___/___

WRITE DOWN ANY STEPS YOU TOOK TOWARDS YOUR GOALS TODAY

REFLECTION:

ONE THING YOU COULD IMPROVE UPON FROM TODAY:

AFFIRMATIONS:

DATE: ___/___/___

EACH AND EVERY DAY IN EACH AND EVERY WAY
MY LIFE IS BETTER AND BETTER

EVENING JOURNALING

DATE: ___/___/___

WRITE DOWN ANY STEPS YOU TOOK TOWARDS YOUR GOALS TODAY

REFLECTION:

ONE THING YOU COULD IMPROVE UPON FROM TODAY:

AFFIRMATIONS:

DATE: ___/___/___

EACH AND EVERY DAY IN EACH AND EVERY WAY
MY LIFE IS BETTER AND BETTER

EVENING JOURNALING

DATE: ___/___/___

WRITE DOWN ANY STEPS YOU TOOK TOWARDS YOUR GOALS TODAY

REFLECTION:

ONE THING YOU COULD IMPROVE UPON FROM TODAY:

AFFIRMATIONS:

DATE: __/__/__

EACH AND EVERY DAY IN EACH AND EVERY WAY
MY LIFE IS BETTER AND BETTER

EVENING JOURNALING

DATE: ___/___/___

WRITE DOWN ANY STEPS YOU TOOK TOWARDS YOUR GOALS TODAY

REFLECTION:

ONE THING YOU COULD IMPROVE UPON FROM TODAY:

AFFIRMATIONS:

DATE: __/__/__

EACH AND EVERY DAY IN EACH AND EVERY WAY
MY LIFE IS BETTER AND BETTER

EVENING JOURNALING

DATE: ___/___/___

WRITE DOWN ANY STEPS YOU TOOK TOWARDS YOUR GOALS TODAY

REFLECTION:

ONE THING YOU COULD IMPROVE UPON FROM TODAY:

AFFIRMATIONS:

DATE: __/__/__

EACH AND EVERY DAY IN EACH AND EVERY WAY
MY LIFE IS BETTER AND BETTER

IT'S TIME TO PAY YOURSELF BY FILLING OUT THIS CHECK!

DATE ____________________

PAY TO THE ORDER OF ____________________ $ [   ]

DOLLARS ____________________

MEMO *I attract abundance* ____________________

0 1 1 0 1 0 0 1 0 2 2 0 1 1 1 1 1 2 2 1 1 4 4 1

Time to celebrate! Write another check to yourself, this time **increasing the amount by 50%** from the balance of your **previous** check.

YOUR SUBCONSCIOUS MIND LOVES WHEN YOU USE MONEY AS A SYMBOL OF YOUR SUCCESS!

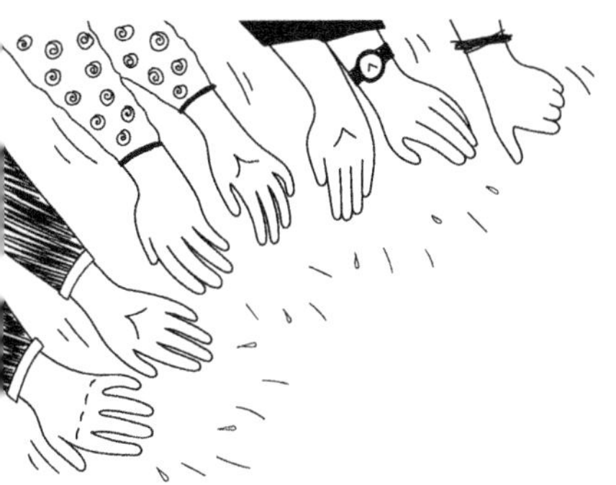

SUCCESS IS ABOUT CREATING A LIFE YOU ARE PROUD OF.

THE DISTANCE BETWEEN DREAMS AND REALITY IS ACTION

EVENING JOURNALING

DATE: ___/___/___

WRITE DOWN ANY STEPS YOU TOOK TOWARDS YOUR GOALS TODAY

REFLECTION:

ONE THING YOU COULD IMPROVE UPON FROM TODAY:

AFFIRMATIONS:

DATE: ___/___/___

EACH AND EVERY DAY IN EACH AND EVERY WAY
MY LIFE IS BETTER AND BETTER

EVENING JOURNALING

DATE: ___/___/___

WRITE DOWN ANY STEPS YOU TOOK TOWARDS YOUR GOALS TODAY

REFLECTION:

ONE THING YOU COULD IMPROVE UPON FROM TODAY:

AFFIRMATIONS:

DATE: __/__/__

EACH AND EVERY DAY IN EACH AND EVERY WAY
MY LIFE IS BETTER AND BETTER

EVENING JOURNALING

DATE: ___/___/___

WRITE DOWN ANY STEPS YOU TOOK TOWARDS YOUR GOALS TODAY

REFLECTION:

ONE THING YOU COULD IMPROVE UPON FROM TODAY:

AFFIRMATIONS:

DATE: __/__/__

EACH AND EVERY DAY IN EACH AND EVERY WAY
MY LIFE IS BETTER AND BETTER

EVENING JOURNALING

DATE: ___/___/___

WRITE DOWN ANY STEPS YOU TOOK TOWARDS YOUR GOALS TODAY

REFLECTION:

ONE THING YOU COULD IMPROVE UPON FROM TODAY:

AFFIRMATIONS: DATE: ___/___/___

EACH AND EVERY DAY IN EACH AND EVERY WAY
MY LIFE IS BETTER AND BETTER

EVENING JOURNALING

DATE: __/__/__

WRITE DOWN ANY STEPS YOU TOOK TOWARDS YOUR GOALS TODAY

REFLECTION:

ONE THING YOU COULD IMPROVE UPON FROM TODAY:

AFFIRMATIONS:

DATE: __/__/__

EACH AND EVERY DAY IN EACH AND EVERY WAY
MY LIFE IS BETTER AND BETTER

EVENING JOURNALING

DATE: ___/___/___

WRITE DOWN ANY STEPS YOU TOOK TOWARDS YOUR GOALS TODAY

REFLECTION:

ONE THING YOU COULD IMPROVE UPON FROM TODAY:

AFFIRMATIONS: DATE: __/__/__

EACH AND EVERY DAY IN EACH AND EVERY WAY
MY LIFE IS BETTER AND BETTER

EVENING JOURNALING

DATE: ___/___/___

WRITE DOWN ANY STEPS YOU TOOK TOWARDS YOUR GOALS TODAY

REFLECTION:

ONE THING YOU COULD IMPROVE UPON FROM TODAY:

AFFIRMATIONS:

DATE: ___/___/___

EACH AND EVERY DAY IN EACH AND EVERY WAY
MY LIFE IS BETTER AND BETTER

IT'S TIME TO PAY YOURSELF BY FILLING OUT THIS CHECK!

DATE

PAY TO THE ORDER OF $

DOLLARS

MEMO *I attract abundance*

0 1 1 0 1 0 0 1 0 2 2 0 1 1 1 1 1 2 2 1 1 4 4 1

Time to celebrate! Write another check to yourself, this time **increasing the amount by 50%** from the balance of your **previous** check.

YOUR SUBCONSCIOUS MIND LOVES WHEN YOU USE MONEY AS A SYMBOL OF YOUR SUCCESS!

BELIEVE IN THE MAGIC INSIDE OF YOU

THE BIGGEST RISK IS NOT TAKING ANY RISK AT ALL

EVENING JOURNALING

DATE: ___/___/___

WRITE DOWN ANY STEPS YOU TOOK TOWARDS YOUR GOALS TODAY

REFLECTION:

ONE THING YOU COULD IMPROVE UPON FROM TODAY:

AFFIRMATIONS:

DATE: ___/___/___

EACH AND EVERY DAY IN EACH AND EVERY WAY
MY LIFE IS BETTER AND BETTER

EVENING JOURNALING

DATE: ___/___/___

WRITE DOWN ANY STEPS YOU TOOK TOWARDS YOUR GOALS TODAY

REFLECTION:

ONE THING YOU COULD IMPROVE UPON FROM TODAY:

AFFIRMATIONS: DATE: ___/___/___

EACH AND EVERY DAY IN EACH AND EVERY WAY
MY LIFE IS BETTER AND BETTER

EVENING JOURNALING

DATE: ___/___/___

WRITE DOWN ANY STEPS YOU TOOK TOWARDS YOUR GOALS TODAY

REFLECTION:

ONE THING YOU COULD IMPROVE UPON FROM TODAY:

AFFIRMATIONS:

DATE: ___/___/___

EACH AND EVERY DAY IN EACH AND EVERY WAY
MY LIFE IS BETTER AND BETTER

EVENING JOURNALING

DATE: ___/___/____

WRITE DOWN ANY STEPS YOU TOOK TOWARDS YOUR GOALS TODAY

REFLECTION:

ONE THING YOU COULD IMPROVE UPON FROM TODAY:

AFFIRMATIONS:

DATE: ___/___/___

EACH AND EVERY DAY IN EACH AND EVERY WAY
MY LIFE IS BETTER AND BETTER

EVENING JOURNALING

DATE: ___/___/___

WRITE DOWN ANY STEPS YOU TOOK TOWARDS YOUR GOALS TODAY

REFLECTION:

ONE THING YOU COULD IMPROVE UPON FROM TODAY:

AFFIRMATIONS:

DATE: ___/___/___

EACH AND EVERY DAY IN EACH AND EVERY WAY
MY LIFE IS BETTER AND BETTER

DATE: ___/___/___

EVENING JOURNALING

WRITE DOWN ANY STEPS YOU TOOK TOWARDS YOUR GOALS TODAY

REFLECTION:

ONE THING YOU COULD IMPROVE UPON FROM TODAY:

AFFIRMATIONS: DATE: ___/___/___

EACH AND EVERY DAY IN EACH AND EVERY WAY
MY LIFE IS BETTER AND BETTER

EVENING JOURNALING

DATE: ___/___/___

WRITE DOWN ANY STEPS YOU TOOK TOWARDS YOUR GOALS TODAY

REFLECTION:

ONE THING YOU COULD IMPROVE UPON FROM TODAY:

AFFIRMATIONS:

DATE: ___/___/___

EACH AND EVERY DAY IN EACH AND EVERY WAY
MY LIFE IS BETTER AND BETTER

IT'S TIME TO PAY YOURSELF BY FILLING OUT THIS CHECK!

DATE

PAY TO THE ORDER OF

$

DOLLARS

MEMO *I attract abundance*

0 1 1 0 1 0 0 1 0 2 2 0 1 1 1 1 1 2 2 1 1 4 4 1

Time to celebrate! Write another check to yourself, this time **increasing the amount by 50%** from the balance of your **previous** check.

YOUR SUBCONSCIOUS MIND LOVES WHEN YOU USE MONEY AS A SYMBOL OF YOUR SUCCESS!

DON'T BE A SPECTATOR IN YOUR LIFE
THE GREATEST DISCOVERY YOU'LL EVER MAKE
IS YOUR OWN POTENTIAL

EVENING JOURNALING

DATE: ___/___/___

WRITE DOWN ANY STEPS YOU TOOK TOWARDS YOUR GOALS TODAY

REFLECTION:

ONE THING YOU COULD IMPROVE UPON FROM TODAY:

AFFIRMATIONS: DATE: ___/___/___

EACH AND EVERY DAY IN EACH AND EVERY WAY
MY LIFE IS BETTER AND BETTER

EVENING JOURNALING

DATE: ___/___/___

WRITE DOWN ANY STEPS YOU TOOK TOWARDS YOUR GOALS TODAY

REFLECTION:

ONE THING YOU COULD IMPROVE UPON FROM TODAY:

AFFIRMATIONS:

DATE: ___/___/___

EACH AND EVERY DAY IN EACH AND EVERY WAY
MY LIFE IS BETTER AND BETTER

EVENING JOURNALING

DATE: ___/___/___

WRITE DOWN ANY STEPS YOU TOOK TOWARDS YOUR GOALS TODAY

REFLECTION:

ONE THING YOU COULD IMPROVE UPON FROM TODAY:

AFFIRMATIONS: DATE: ___/___/___

EACH AND EVERY DAY IN EACH AND EVERY WAY
MY LIFE IS BETTER AND BETTER

EVENING JOURNALING

DATE: ___/___/___

WRITE DOWN ANY STEPS YOU TOOK TOWARDS YOUR GOALS TODAY

REFLECTION:

ONE THING YOU COULD IMPROVE UPON FROM TODAY:

AFFIRMATIONS: DATE: ___/___/___

EACH AND EVERY DAY IN EACH AND EVERY WAY
MY LIFE IS BETTER AND BETTER

EVENING JOURNALING

DATE: ___/___/___

WRITE DOWN ANY STEPS YOU TOOK TOWARDS YOUR GOALS TODAY

REFLECTION:

ONE THING YOU COULD IMPROVE UPON FROM TODAY:

AFFIRMATIONS:

DATE: ___/___/___

EACH AND EVERY DAY IN EACH AND EVERY WAY
MY LIFE IS BETTER AND BETTER

EVENING JOURNALING

DATE: __/__/__

WRITE DOWN ANY STEPS YOU TOOK TOWARDS YOUR GOALS TODAY

REFLECTION:

ONE THING YOU COULD IMPROVE UPON FROM TODAY:

AFFIRMATIONS: DATE: ___/___/___

EACH AND EVERY DAY IN EACH AND EVERY WAY
MY LIFE IS BETTER AND BETTER

EVENING JOURNALING

DATE: ___/___/___

WRITE DOWN ANY STEPS YOU TOOK TOWARDS YOUR GOALS TODAY

REFLECTION:

ONE THING YOU COULD IMPROVE UPON FROM TODAY:

AFFIRMATIONS:

DATE: ___/___/___

EACH AND EVERY DAY IN EACH AND EVERY WAY
MY LIFE IS BETTER AND BETTER

IT'S TIME TO PAY YOURSELF BY FILLING OUT THIS CHECK!

DATE ______________________

PAY TO THE ORDER OF ______________________ $ ________

DOLLARS ______________________

MEMO *I attract abundance* ______________________

0 1 1 0 1 0 0 1 0 2 2 0 1 1 1 1 1 2 2 1 1 4 4 1

Time to celebrate! Write another check to yourself, this time **increasing the amount by 50%** from the balance of your **previous** check.

YOUR SUBCONSCIOUS MIND LOVES WHEN YOU USE MONEY AS A SYMBOL OF YOUR SUCCESS!

CONGRATULATIONS ON COMPLETING THE MANIFESTATION BLUEPRINT!

You've taken a significant step in transforming your dreams into reality, and that's something to celebrate. As you close this chapter, remember: the journey doesn't end here. Every page you've filled, every affirmation you've written and every action you've taken is part of your ongoing transformation.

But what's next? Now is the time to continue building momentum. Keep journaling, keep visualizing, and most importantly, keep believing in the power within you. It's time to pick up another copy of this book to carry on your journey—whether for yourself or as a gift to someone you care about. There's something magical about filling out its pages, knowing that each word, each intention brings you closer to your goals.

As you move forward, I invite you to visit www.GlennRottmann.com which is also the home of **The Hypno Vault**. You'll find additional resources, tools, and products designed to support your continued growth. Whether you need more guidance, inspiration, or new ways to engage with your manifestation practice, it's all there waiting for you.

Remember: consistency creates miracles. You have the power to create a life that reflects your highest dreams. Keep going, **stay committed, and trust the process**. You are capable of more than you have ever realized, and your potential is limitless!

SCAN THE QR CODES TO CONTINUE YOUR JOURNEY. JOIN THE HYPNO VAULT AND REORDER YOUR MANIFESTATION BLUEPRINT JOURNAL—YOUR GROWTH IS JUST BEGINNING.

THE HYPNO VAULT

REORDER NOW

STAY INSPIRED, STAY EMPOWERED AND ABOVE ALL KEEP MANIFESTING!

~GLENN ROTTMANN

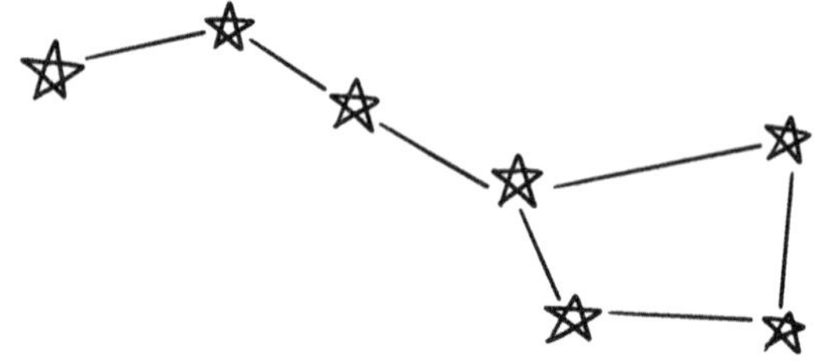

Author: Glenn Rottmann
Illustrator: Erica Fraticelli
Editor: Oliva Rottmann
Back cover artwork
"Universal Light": Amber Evans

Printed in Dunstable, United Kingdom